Preparing for Parenthood

Preparing for Parenthood

GRACE KETTERMAN, M.D.

BEACON HILL PRESS OF KANSAS CITY
Kansas City, Missouri

Copyright 1996
by Beacon Hill Press of Kansas City

ISBN 083-411-6197

Printed in the
United States of America

Cover Design: Mike Walsh

Cover Photo: Tony Stone Images

10   9   8   7   6   5   4   3   2   1

Contents

Introduction

In today's Western culture many couples have decided they cannot manage the vicissitudes of parenting. They choose to have no children, and medical discoveries have enabled them to avoid pregnancy safely. I deeply respect individuals' rights to decide what is right for them. But I confess that I feel sorry for such couples. When I am with my children and grandchildren, the joy and warmth of our intimacy is indescribable. I wish everyone could experience this kind of communication.

If you are considering remaining childless, I urge you to think ahead. Being free of the responsibility and expense of a family may seem wonderful right now, but how will it be when you are 50 or 60? Envision your holidays with no excited squeals from the youngsters who might bring fun to your festivities. Imagine a solitude that would never be broken by the companionship of adult children.

Those of you who do choose to have a family sometimes go to the other end of life's spectrum. You may believe there's nothing much to having and raising children. People have been doing it since the dawn of creation. You may put little if any consideration into the preparation for adding a child to your marriage.

Now somewhere between these two extremes is the thoughtful middle of the spectrum. Yes, you think, we do want children, but we know that we must be ready to provide the right environment for them. Furthermore, you realize that our culture is one that does not help us a great deal in the challenging task of raising healthy kids. How can you prepare to face this immense responsibility with confidence and joy?

This book is my attempt to help you answer this very crucial question. You can discover if you are ready to have a child. If not, you can learn how to prepare yourselves. You can create a climate that is conducive to rearing children who will bring you joy and who can mature into productive, healthy adults.

1

Preparing Physically

You may be one of those couples who blithely decide one day to have a child. Perhaps your best friends have a new baby, and they can speak of nothing else. He seems to be so charming as you've watched him learn to smile and patty-cake, so you think it would be nice to have one too.

It may indeed be wonderful to add a child to your family. Or it may be disastrous. The difference may be in the temperament type of the child you are given. But far more, the difference will depend on whether or not you are ready.

Let's begin by considering your physical health. Babies deserve the best possible start in life. You can provide that by being sure both of you are in the best possible shape.

Avoiding Toxic Chemicals

I'm not talking about your measurements, but your basic level of fitness. You probably know the risks that tobacco and alcohol create for a developing fetus. You may not realize, however, that at the time of conception the risk factors are just as true for fathers as for mothers. Unfortunately, the use of these chemicals has become increasingly common in Christian families.

If you are considering conceiving a new life, by all means dispense with the use of alcohol and tobacco.

Mothers, during your pregnancy, it is crucial that you avoid these chemicals. It may be awkward to ask others to stop smoking when you are in a meeting or at a social event. But secondhand smoke is toxic. Avoid it. Find a gracious way to excuse yourself, or ask others to be considerate of you.

Hopefully you are not addicted to illegal drugs, but it is common for people to take prescription drugs. Some of these could damage a newly conceived baby. Be sure to ask your doctor if there is any risk. If there is, unless your medication is necessary for your survival, I suggest you stop using it. Consult your physician about how to do so. Some medications can be stopped abruptly, whereas others should be gradually decreased.

Weight Control

The pendulum swing on weight control is a wide one. When I was having my children four decades ago, doctors rigidly forbade gaining more than 20 pounds. If I exceeded the allotted weight gain for a given month, I was soundly reprimanded and put on a strict diet. Later a highly permissive philosophy invaded our culture. Doctors no longer worried about weight gains, and 40 or more pounds could be put on with no apparent concern.

Much more recently the medical profession has focused on the problems of obesity. Many women have discovered that the excessive pounds gained during a pregnancy were the beginning of a weight problem.

I'm an advocate of common sense and moderation. Obesity is a major threat to good health. If your weight has climbed to more than 10 percent above your ideal weight, you need to reduce it before conception. Trying to lose weight rapidly while attempting to get pregnant is probably not a good idea, though. Lose weight slowly, using a healthful diet. Try to get close to your ideal weight, and then maintain it in the weeks before and during conception.

Your ideal weight may be estimated using the following formula: At 5 feet in height, the ideal weight is 100 pounds. For each inch over that height, add 5 pounds. If you are 5 feet 5 inches, you should weigh 125 pounds. Most authorities would add 10 percent of that to your total weight and not worry.

While this weight issue is crucial for mothers, prospective fathers can make it easier by joining in a healthful eating regimen. It's really important that fathers stay healthy so they will have the energy to share in the care of the new child.

Healthful Eating Habits

We live in a highly nutrition-conscious world, perhaps excessively so. As God's children we have a responsibility to our Creator to be as healthy as is reasonably possible. Develop good, balanced dietary habits. Every public library and bookstore is stocked with information regarding healthful eating. Scan a few books, but let common sense be your guide.

Everyone needs some of the following foods daily:

1. *Grain derivatives,* such as cereal and bread. Some authorities state you need two to seven pounds weekly, depending on your activity and metabolic levels.
2. *Dairy products,* including milk and cheese. We know that animal fats contain cholesterol, so you need to use low-fat products. These are readily available in your local supermarket.
3. *Meat,* including fish, poultry, and beef. Fish and poultry generally have less cholesterol. Broiling meats and draining off the fat also reduces cholesterol. Your doctor can do studies of your blood that will let you know how much you are at risk

for damaging levels of cholesterol. Some people prefer to eat little or no meat. They eat cheese and more vegetables in the beans-legume family to get their protein requirements.

4. *Citrus fruits,* including oranges, grapefruit, lemons, and limes. These are an important source of vitamin C and fiber. You need two and a half to five pounds weekly.

5. *Potatoes,* a surprisingly good source of vitamin C and the carbohydrate starch, which we all need as an energy source. Only if you put a great deal of butter or sour cream on them do they become a very fattening food. You need two to five pounds a week.

6. *Leafy green and yellow vegetables,* which are needed in the amount of three and a half to five pounds weekly. These provide fiber, a range of vitamins, and are usually enjoyable to eat.

7. *Other fruits and vegetables,* which include a host of items your appetite can dictate. You need three to six pounds weekly. These may include apples, grapes, berries, and melons. Peas, green beans, okra, and eggplant are only a few of the vegetables you may like.

8. *Eggs.* You need six or seven a week. They may be put into puddings or boiled and chopped into a salad if you don't like them. Eggs have gained a bad reputation because of their cholesterol content, but recent studies reveal that we need some of this substance. There are efforts by breeders to create strains of chickens that produce lower-cholesterol-content eggs. The final answer lies in your doctor's studies of your family history and your own body's chemistry.

9. *Dried beans, peas, lentils, and nuts.* These should

contribute only two to four ounces of your weekly diet. So you may have peanut butter on your toast now and then!

10. *Vitamins and minerals.* These are invisible chemicals that are present in the foods just listed. Since many of today's foods are processed, they become unreliable as sources of the vitamins we need. I feel that a simple vitamin-mineral tablet daily is a wise habit before and during pregnancy as well as when nursing a new baby.

You need to drink at least eight glasses of water daily. Learn to limit caffeine-containing drinks, and I suggest you avoid the excess sugar and sweeteners in the list of sodas we all drink and enjoy but do not need.

Exercise

It seems that many Americans go to some extremes in the area of exercise. Many people exercise off even the healthy layer of fat we need for winter warmth and calorie reserves. Others store up fat as if there were no food for tomorrow. Current research reveals that genetic factors make gaining weight easier for many of us. I always panic just a bit at such information. You can easily come to believe that you are helpless to cope with weight problems because they are from your parents' genes. This idea is just not true!

Certainly those of us who have had obese parents will struggle more to overcome weight gain than others. But good, regular exercise, along with healthy eating habits, will hold your weight to just where it needs to be.

How much you need to exercise depends on your metabolic rate (how rapidly your body burns up calories) and your food intake. It also depends on your daily work. If your job keeps you moving a great deal, you will need less planned exercise than if you sit at a desk most of the day.

I suggest you start with 10 to 20 minutes of exercise daily until your weight becomes stable. If you need to lose some pounds, increase this time by 5 minutes a day until you reach the time it takes to lose and level off. You shouldn't have a weight problem if you follow this practice of balancing exercise and food intake to maintain health.

It makes sense to me to choose the kind of exercise before pregnancy that you can follow during gestation. Walking is the most universally available form of exercising. A brisk pace that requires deep breathing and makes your heart pump vigorously is the ideal degree of exercise. Swimming may appeal to you, and if this is possible and your doctor approves of it during pregnancy, swim away. Exercise gyms are popular, and many have trained instructors to assist you. Be sure to find out, when you become pregnant, whether these kinds of activities are too strenuous.

It's not easy to form good exercise habits. During bad weather you will hate to get out and maintain your routine. Do it anyway! Disciplining yourself to maintain good physical care will also help you become a more mature, self-controlled parent later.

Rest

I am a person who craves rest. It is very difficult for me to exercise and control my eating habits. But after a long and disciplined day, I can go to bed with a good conscience and great pleasure. My bed becomes my reward for that difficult day's performance. I have my own little routine that includes a small, well-focused reading lamp and a good book. I may be able to peruse 5 pages or sometimes 50 before I fall asleep. But to me, rest is a reward.

You may find rest to be boring. Life may be so exciting that you hate taking time out to sleep. Or your life may be so difficult that you sleep to escape. Once again, I urge you to seek a balance. The average amount of sleep most people need is eight hours.

If you plan to try to get pregnant, you really need to get enough sleep to keep you from being tired. You should awaken refreshed enough to cope with your day and keep active until bedtime. I can hear some of you say, "No matter how early I go to bed, I'm never ready to get up!" Believe me, I understand that. I'm not a morning person. But let me assure you: most babies *are!* Get your days and nights in order if you plan to become parents.

Positive Attitude

The Bible says, "As he thinks in his heart, so is he" (Prov. 23:7, NKJV). Scripture admonishes us to be our best by dwelling on "whatever things are true . . . noble . . . just . . . pure . . . lovely . . . of good report, . . . meditate on these" (Phil. 4:8, NKJV). Forming the fine art of positive thinking improves our total health. Developing an affirming attitude is one of the strengths of wholesome individuals and families.

So now you know how to be physically well. You will be well along in your preparation to become good parents when you turn these truths into habits. Go for it!

Expectant Parents' Journal

Chapter 1

Getting in Touch

My *feelings* upon learning I was pregnant were _____

My *thoughts* about being pregnant are _____

_____

Healthful Lifestyle Report Card

Give yourself and your spouse a letter grade (A-F) on these areas addressed in chapter 1:

	You	*Spouse*
Toxic chemicals	_____	_____
Weight	_____	_____
Eating habits	_____	_____
Exercise	_____	_____
Rest	_____	_____
Positive attitude	_____	_____

List three specific actions you can take this week to improve your expectant parents grade point average:

1.

2.

3.

If you are listening, little one . . .
(Write a message to your unborn child.)

_____

_____

Medical Matters

My major health concern for myself during this pregnancy is ___

_____

Questions I will ask my doctor relating to this concern for myself
are _____

_____

My major health concern for my baby during this pregnancy is

_____

Questions I will ask my doctor relating to this concern for my baby are _____

_____

_____

Checkup!

According to the author's formula, my ideal weight is _____ lbs.

5' =   100 lbs.

+5 lbs. for every inch more =   _____ lbs. (give or take 10
    percent)

Which of the following foods did you eat yesterday?

Grains	_____	Citrus fruits	_____
Dairy products	_____	Potatoes	_____
Meat	_____	Leafy green/yellow vegetables	_____
Eggs	_____	Other fruits and vegetables	_____
Vitamin tablet	_____	Beans, peas, lentils, nuts	_____

Fill in the blanks:

Yesterday I drank _____ glasses of water, _____ drinks containing caffeine, and _____ drinks containing excess sugar or sweeteners.

Today/tomorrow I will drink _____ glasses of water, _____ drinks containing caffeine, and _____ drinks containing excess sugar or sweeteners.

Yesterday I exercised _____ minutes when I engaged in the following activity: _____.

Today/tomorrow I will exercise for _____ minutes when I engage in the following activity: _____.

Notes

(Jot down any thoughts this chapter triggered, including questions you would like to ask your relatives about family medical history, advice from your doctor about an exercise plan, and so on.)

2

Maturity

A grief-stricken father once said to me concerning his daughter, "Julie is 20. She's away at college. She ought to be mature enough to take care of herself!"

Julie had just announced that she was pregnant, unmarried, and not at all prepared to raise a child. Her father's words became indelibly embedded in my memory, because they were so obvious but so false.

Achieving a certain age or status in life does not at all mean that one is mature. Maturity is a growing process that takes place when each developmental stage is completed appropriately. Each new level, built on the solid foundations beneath, brings one closer to this coveted state—maturity.

Here are some of the qualities that can help you define the degree of your maturity.

Goals

"Jeannie," I asked, "what do you plan to be doing 10 years from now?" Her downcast brown eyes were veiled by her long black hair. The droop of her shoulders and the unsmiling mouth revealed the profound sadness of her 16 years. Jeannie's family loved her and had provided well for her, but she had rebelled against their rules and unbending strictness. Jeannie became immersed in a daily battle against her parents that was fast being lost by all of them.

I hoped to help her see that all too soon she would be independent, choosing for herself the life she would lead. Jeannie had no idea what her future might hold and no goals of her own.

In today's fast-paced world, I find very few young people who establish goals. Both short- and long-range goals are not a part of their thoughts or plans. Because of the extremes of parenting—permissive or overly strict (like Jeannie's)—children grow to an adult age with a major weakness. They do not recognize their God-given talents and fail to perceive where these may lead them. Without goals, life becomes meaningless, futile.

One study I read revealed that seriously depressed individuals became better when they completed one task daily. It might be as simple as neatly making a bed or washing up yesterday's dirty dishes, but they felt better by doing it.

I urge you to begin now. Establish attainable goals—daily, weekly, monthly, and for your entire life. Daily goals may well include a regular schedule of work and play, completing jobs for each day. Some tasks and fun activities need to be done weekly. Cleaning the garage or storage areas or keeping up your lawn are common tasks. Remember to intersperse some fun with your work, so plan a hike, picnic, or evening with your spouse or friends. Once a month, at least, arrange for a big play or work project that will bring you a sense of pride and well-being.

How few couples plan for the long range! Yet every family hopes to see their children launched into a successful life. Plan ahead to provide for times of crisis such as job loss or illness, and certainly old age. Many couples never consider a will or arrange for estate planning. Mature couples plan for the future.

Balance

Being a good parent is not convenient. It is instead a constant challenge to avoid damaging extremes and to establish healthy balance. One of the core needs of every child is the need for consistency or predictability. By your own inborn personality, you may find this to be easy or very difficult. Whatever it takes, develop this balance.

Let me give you an example. Sally was by nature a driven, organized, even rigid person. Her husband, Hal, in stark contrast was a peace-loving, easy mark for his wife's strong-willed, manipulative personality. As a child, Sally had resented her mom's rigid standards, realizing she could never measure up. On the other hand, she had little respect for her dad's passivity and gullibility. On either hand, she had lived in guilt and anger. She married a man much like her father and learned later it was difficult to respect him as well. Her whole life had lacked balance.

What this young lady needed was a degree of flexibility in a basically fair and logical climate of predictability. Balance was missing.

If you want to become wise parents, you need to learn how to balance rigidity with flexibility to create consistency. The product will be a fair and reasonable environment in which your child can learn wisdom from you and God and develop his or her own maturity.

The great asset in having two parents is that each offers balance to the other. Of course, this demands that each is secure enough to exchange helpful criticisms with the other without becoming defensive or feeling inadequate.

Integrity

This character quality implies attributes of honesty and security. A person of integrity knows and likes himself or herself. The root word for "integrity" is "integer," meaning one, the whole.

When you can love yourself as God loves you—unconditionally—you are nearly there. When you are whole, complete in God and yourself, you won't care so much about another's criticism. You will in fact learn to welcome it so you can improve and grow. Only when you become your own independent, whole person are you ready for marriage. You will be able to enter a relationship of inter-dependence successfully when you accept your weaknesses and strengths, as well as those of your spouse.

What a team two parents can become when they understand and practice this quality of integrity! During a counseling session in my office, Jim recently said to his wife, Ellen, "Honey, you expect too much of me! I can't stop working on my computer to talk to you every few minutes!"

Ellen promptly dissolved into tears, then clenched her fists and yelled, "There you go again! You never have time for me! You don't care about me at all! Why did I ever marry you?" I could tell this was an oft-repeated drama reenacted by both of them.

Had either of them been a truly whole person, that dialogue would have gone like this: Jim would have said, "Ellen, I'm so blessed to have you for my wife! I'm so glad you want my love!" He would give her a quick hug and continue, "Give me 30 minutes, I'll finish my work, and we can relax by the TV or go for a walk."

Ellen in turn would have said, "You're a great husband. You know, after this I won't interrupt you—so you can finish your work even faster!"

Which way do you want to live? To become integrated and mature, you must

1. unconditionally accept yourself and others;
2. admit your weaknesses and work at strengthening them—in other words, accept reality;
3. accept others' criticisms without defensiveness but with gratitude that they care about your growth;

4. give criticism to others lovingly so they can change and grow with you;
5. be self-sufficient enough that you can sense your spouse's feelings and needs at least as acutely as you do your own;
6. have enough inner resources to support and help others without robbing yourself;
7. be capable of enjoying *giving* more than *getting;*
8. be able to relate with others in consistent ways, creating mutual joy and security.

I'm certain you can see how priceless these qualities are in your marriage. They are even more crucial when you become parents.

Postponement of Present Pleasure

One of the most reliable indicators of maturity is the ability to postpone present pleasure in order to serve the interest of future good. For several decades a popular bumper sticker read, "If it feels good, do it!" The instant gratification of impulsive desires and the uncontrolled expression of every feeling became more than slogans over the years. People actually lived by them.

Though there has been some swinging of that pendulum, there are still vestiges of the hedonism of immaturity. In raising a child, as in building a healthy marriage, there are many times when your desires and sometimes even your needs must be put on hold.

Once again, let me remind you to seek a balance in this whole concept. If you go too long with excessive deprivation of your needs, you can become emotionally bankrupt and even physically ill. Take care of yourself, but be prepared for a period of time to sacrifice some of your pleasure for the greater good of your entire family.

Adaptation to Change

If you thought marriage transformed your lifestyle, you were right! But I can hardly think of a word that describes accurately the magnitude of change a child brings into the family. Every aspect of your life is slammed into an immensely different cycle. Your sleep will be rudely interrupted by the baby's hunger. Eating with both hands free is usually impossible as you cradle a crying infant in one arm. Going out impulsively for coffee or lunch with friends demands packing a weekend bag!

You had better plan to adapt to variations in life now. You may have been born with a temperament that thrives on predictability, and for you this adjustment will become a trial. But about the only thing you can rely on with a baby is the *un*predictability that is born with him or her.

I suggest the following ideas to help you cope with the inevitable change a child brings into your life.

1. Borrow a baby from someone you know for an evening or a weekend. Your friends will love the respite, and you can live with the hands-on changes to which you will need to adjust. Be aware, of course, that the baby *you* will have will be a much better one!

2. Practice doing some impulsive things, such as arising at sunrise for a long hike. Getting up to feed the baby won't be that difficult!

3. Invite guests for dinner or dessert when you may not exactly feel like it. Your baby will need meals when you are downright ill.

4. Practice dividing your attention to each other in order to do a major project. One of the toughest parts of having a baby is that he or she will need you at times when you most need each other. By the way, be sure that reaching out to your spouse's needs,

like meeting your own, is not canceled—only postponed.

5. One of the most difficult assignments of new parents is the often necessary postponement of sexual intimacy. You will benefit from creative thinking and good humor in order to achieve time for sex without interruption. But this too will pass. Be wise enough to avoid placing blame and becoming grouchy when you have to wait even for days at a time.

The Capacity to Love and Be Loved

You may think the capacity to love and be loved is a foolish expression. Of course you love, and certainly you crave being loved. Randall and Kim thought so too. But when he wanted to hug her or tickle her while she was preparing dinner, she roughly shoved him away and rudely asked if he couldn't see that she was busy—and busy fixing his dinner, for crying out loud! Kim was in no mood to make love that evening.

Unfortunately, marital love has been considered to be a gooey, sexual feeling. If that feeling dissolves, people commonly believe they are no longer *in* love. Love, especially to Christians, is far more than a feeling. It is a decision, a commitment, and a living out of God's love in us. Feelings vary, depending on health, fatigue, and personal disagreements. Don't live by feeling, but by a rational, decision-making philosophy.

Children will try your patience to its limits at times. If you do not respond lovingly, you will add to their distress. Always remember the three faces of love—tender, tough, and protective. By keeping each interwoven with the others, your love will be balanced, successfully bonding your family together.

I want to share with you a vignette in which I experienced a way to *be* loving when I *felt* most *un*loving. Early in our marriage I found myself feeling put-upon. I worked very hard in my profession and then was faced with the management of a household and three children, each with differing needs. My husband worked very hard also, but when he returned home, he could relax and do his own thing.

One day I staged a first-rate pity party and progressed from feeling sorry for myself to being downright angry at my spouse. I wanted to walk away, but I knew how such decisions often end. "How would I treat him if I felt loving toward him?" I asked myself. The answer was clear because I had done so many times.

I fixed his favorite dinner and greeted his "Daddy's home!" announcement with a hug. Before I knew it, my feeling of love was back. By the way, I learned to negotiate a more fair sharing of the work as well. Both tender and tough love must be balanced to protect a relationship.

Responsibility

Mature people must evidence the quality of being responsible. This means you do with reasonable promptness the jobs that need to be done. You do them to the best of your ability, and you complete them as quickly as possible.

Responsibility also includes the ability to make wise decisions. You recall the concept of postponing present pleasure for future good? If you must decide how to budget your income, for example, can you do so considering the welfare of your entire family? Or do you think primarily of your own desires and interests?

Responsible thinking, deciding, and acting demand these steps:

1. Take time to gather information. Be sure you listen to others' experiences, read about situations similar to yours, and think of as many facts as possible regarding situations you may face.

2. Compile a list of all the possible options a given event may include. The classic lists of pros and cons are always useful.
3. When you have as much information and as many comparisons as you can reasonably collect, and your possible options are listed, make your decision. This may at times be frightening. Maturity enables you to take that risk and finalize the choice. (Throughout this list "you" means both husband and wife.)
4. Live with the consequences. If the outcome of your choice was positive, rejoice without gloating. This can be tough if your spouse disagreed with you. If by chance your decision resulted in a disaster, don't wallow in remorse and guilt. Learn whatever lessons you can, avoid repeating that mistake, and move on.

Review these steps, considering their application to raising a child you might have. I suspect you will readily see that the struggle of mastering responsibility will pay great dividends.

Practice those skills of self-control, unselfishness, and finding the long-range perspectives of life. You *can* make wise decisions that will help you become a mature person. Your child will love you for it, and your future will be blessed because of your efforts.

Expectant Parents' Journal

Chapter 2

Getting in Touch

My *feelings* about being a parent are _____

_____

My *thoughts* about being a parent are _____

_____

Ready or Not, It's Time to Grow Up!

Look over these topics treated in chapter 2, "Maturity." Put a plus (+) by the two maturity factors you believe are the strongest in your life. Put a minus (-) next to the two factors you need to work on the most.

Marks of Maturity Checklist

_____ Goal setting   _____ Adapting to change

_____ Balance   _____ Loving and being loved

_____ Integrity   _____ Responsibility

_____ Postponing present pleasures

What definite steps are you going to take this week to improve those areas you marked with a minus? Be specific. _____

_____

_____

If you are listening, little one . . .
(Write a message to your unborn child.)

_____

_____

For Inspiration
*The LORD called me from the womb, from the body of
my mother he named my name* (Isa. 49:1, RSV).

One-Sentence Prayers
A prayer for my baby: _____

_____

_____

_____

A prayer for my spouse: _____

_____

_____

A prayer for myself: _____

_____

_____

Checkup!

Reread Dr. Ketterman's comments on setting *attainable* goals. Complete the inventory below:

Two of my life goals are _____

_____

Two of my personal goals for this year are _____

_____

My monthly goals include _____

_____

My weekly goals include _____

_____

My daily goals include _____

_____

Interact

The three most common areas of friction in my marriage are

a.

b.

c.

The weaknesses I have that contribute to this friction are

a.

b.

c.

Specific actions I can take to improve these weaknesses are

a.

b.

c.

Pray now about the items listed above. If you feel comfortable in doing so, invite your spouse to join you in prayer. Remember—the focus here is your weaknesses, not your mate's!

Notes

3

Economic Readiness

Jan and Ben were anxious to have a child. They married after college, when they were in their mid-20s. She had a job as a teacher, while Ben was still facing several years in graduate school. On her modest salary, the couple budgeted carefully to keep from incurring even more debt than they already owed for educational loans.

Both Ben and Jan had grown up in comfortable homes, with all of their needs and most of their wants provided by loving, successful parents. Their neighborhoods were not affluent, but certainly lovely.

Now they wanted exactly such an environment for their children. But they lived in a cramped apartment in the university housing unit. There were too many people around, and the area was noisy and cluttered. If they waited for Ben to finish grad school, they would be nearly 30, and they knew that conception might be more difficult in that age bracket.

Jan and Ben's dilemma is shared by a great many thoughtful and responsible couples. Perhaps you are among them. Let's discuss some commonsense ideas to help guide you economically.

1. *Babies need and deserve one of their parents to care for them during those crucial early months.* Can you

manage on one person's income to provide adequately, if not affluently?

2. *Babies couldn't care less whether they live in a mansion or a tiny apartment.* They just need parents who adore them, love each other, and maintain a safe, hygienic environment. Later, children need a neighborhood with good playmates and a reasonably safe social climate.

3. *Children never need designer clothing or expensive equipment.* A couple I admire makes furniture, toys, and play equipment at little cost. Creating toys from cardboard cartons, for example, can be fun for the entire family.

4. *Remember again that parenting is not convenient.* You can deny yourselves much of the spending of money that you would enjoy in order to provide for your child.

It doesn't require a great deal of money to care adequately for young children. But it is crucial that you manage your money well and avoid some common pitfalls.

1. *Don't fight over money.* To prevent anxiety and fighting over money, you need basic financial security. That means your income must cover the bare-bones costs of living, including rent, utilities, transportation, clothing, food, taxes, and health care costs.

2. *Analyze all aspects of your economy.* Look for safe but economic housing—no small challenge. Watch your energy expenditures. You can stand a little cooler or warmer temperatures without great discomfort in order to save on utility costs. You may find that insuring yourselves will save a great deal of money on health insurance. One family I knew put into a savings account the money they would have lost in a large company's health in-

surance costs. They came out financially well ahead. I don't recommend that if you are not healthy, cautious people, or if you work in a risky environment. It is a plan a few families have found to provide well for their needs, but *it is risky.*

3. *Be sure to save as much as possible.* Putting money aside is difficult for most of us. A well-known banker in my city once said the average upper-income family in our town could survive financially without an income for a maximum of only three months. Yet it is not uncommon for a person to lose a job and be out of work for a year or more. Save enough to be monetarily secure for as long as possible if you are planning to have a child.

4. *Seek financial counsel from someone who is knowledgeable but also has your interest at heart.* Buying a home seems more advisable than losing the amount you pay in rent every month. A recent article I read, however, challenged that idea with valid reasons. So think carefully, collect information thoroughly, and decide wisely about all major expenditures.

5. *Avoid using credit cards as much as possible.* You will pay excessively high interest rates and create burdensome financial stress for your family. Try to pay for every purchase when you make it, or at least pay by the end of each month to prevent those interest losses. I am amazed at credit card companies who freely offer ever-increasing maximum amounts of available credit. It seems so simple to go ahead and use it, but before you know it, you are buried in debt.

6. *Learn to live as simply as is compatible with your current status.* Many years ago that guiding phi-

losophy became my personal motto. The old "keeping up with the Joneses" competition has no place in the Christian's economy. This motto may move you to learn how to repair broken items, sew, cook, and keep up your surroundings to create loveliness at low cost. Such activities, in fact, can make a team out of your family and can be fun as well as an economic saving.

7. *Create a budget that will fit your family, and discipline yourselves to maintain it.* I prefer budgets that are a bit flexible and bearable but that are tight enough to challenge your spending limits. Ours is an acquisitional culture—"If you really want it, buy it!" Yet many of the things we think we need are actually luxuries, and most of the items we want we could very well do without. Be sure in a budget that you allot a bit of "mad money" for each of you. We all need a little financial independence. Try to give each other absolute freedom with that money, but equally hold each other kindly accountable for the rest of the budget.

8. *Review your budget at least twice a year.* Your needs and income will change regularly, and this fact will influence your budget. We saw in chapter 2 that mature people must adapt to change. Having a child will bring unexpected changes in your expenditures almost weekly for the majority of your life.

9. *Long-range financial planning is vital.* As insecure as all of us in the United States feel about Social Security retirement benefits, we dare not count on that alone to meet the needs of old age. On the other hand, the needs of an expanding family consume most, if not all, of the average monthly

income. I urge you to put at least a tiny bit of money into a retirement fund monthly. If you can keep this as safe as if you didn't even have it, you will be surprised at its growth rate over time. You may be able to increase such savings if your income grows. It's been my experience that spending increases precisely as income grows. You can prevent that, or at least hold it to a minimum, by a carefully followed savings plan.

10. *Read the advice of Christian economists.* They all recommend tithing your income. The Bible is explicit about commanding our giving to God of that sacrificial tithe. At times it seems impossible, but the people who obey this command report God blesses them and enables them to live comfortably on the rest.

Material Needs of a Baby

In a local drugstore window, a very plain-looking plastic high chair is priced at $175. To me that is a huge amount of money for an item that will be used only two years or less—if it doesn't break first. You can pay exorbitant amounts of money on infant furniture. It's tempting to think, Our baby deserves the very best! And, of course, he or she does. But what *is* the best?

Let me strongly recommend that you explore the world of garage sales and used baby items, often barely used. A good cleaning or a coat of fresh paint can restore these to pieces that will see several children through infancy.

Infants' wearing apparel can also be found at very little cost in garage sales. A careful laundering can provide a fine layette for pennies. My experience has been that infants outgrow tiny sizes sooner than labels suggest, so purchase slightly larger sizes that your baby can grow into.

In my church there are many younger couples who

smartly exchange baby clothes and equipment. Maternity clothes, too, can often be borrowed if you provide good care and return them in excellent condition (or pass them on to someone else).

Nursing your baby provides another opportunity to economize. Baby formulas are many. They are adequate for baby's needs, but they are costly. Nursing your baby is by far the best for him or her in most ways and is much cheaper. Furthermore, if you eat carefully, it can help you give up some of your body's excess calories so your weight will return to normal more quickly.

Diapers are another costly item for babies. The wonderful disposable ones are so convenient that most parents insist on them. If you can afford them, by all means use them. But if you *really* need to economize, cloth diapers are your answer. You must wash them, as all baby's wearing apparel, in a mild soap and use double rinsing to avoid irritating your infant's tender skin. If they need bleaching at times, do so as carefully as possible, and then run them through a full washing cycle to prevent irritation from the bleach.

In order to be economically ready for a child, you probably will have to change your lifestyle. You will find this especially true and most difficult if both of you have had good incomes and enjoyed living it up. The changes you make need to be done gladly, even joyfully, for the sake of having and caring well for a child. If you find yourself chafing under your constricted financial situation, it is very likely you will grow to resent your child. Children are quick to sense such a feeling. Recognize the eternal worth of a child—*your* child—and it will become possible for you to avoid such resentment.

While you can make it much easier on yourselves economically by waiting until your financial situation is ideal, if that takes too long, it may not be wise. Don't wait until you are too old to find the energy to enjoy your child, but don't rush into childbearing before you have some security and a workable plan for managing your family's needs.

Expectant Parents' Journal

Chapter 3

Getting in Touch

My *feelings* about my baby's material needs are _____

_____

My *thoughts* about our financial situation are _____

_____

Money Management Inventory

On a continuum of 1-10 (1 is terrible, 5 is average, 10 is excellent), rate your money managing as a couple. When you've completed the inventory, ask your spouse to do so. Compare answers and dialogue on ways to improve low scores.

You	Spouse	
_____	_____	We don't fight over money.
_____	_____	We analyze all aspects of our economy.
_____	_____	We save as much as possible.
_____	_____	If needed, we seek financial counsel from a knowledgeable person we both trust.
_____	_____	We avoid using credit cards as much as possible.
_____	_____	We live as simply as is compatible with our current status.

_____	_____ We designed a budget, and we live within it.
_____	_____ We review our budget at least twice a year.
_____	_____ We have long-range financial plans.
_____	_____ We read the advice of Christian economists.

If you are listening, little one . . .
(Write a message to your unborn child.)

_____

_____

Checkup!
Check the following essentials your baby still needs:

_____ diapers (4 dozen cloth, 6 dozen disposable to begin with)

_____ 3-7 undershirts

_____ 3-7 sleepers

_____ 2-4 pairs booties or socks

_____ 3-7 outfits (depending on time of year)

_____ 2-6 crib sheets

_____ 1-2 crib-size blankets

_____ 4-6 receiving blankets

_____ 2-4 washable bibs

_____ crib with mattress and bumper pads

_____ car seat

_____ diaper bag

_____ stroller (optional)

_____ baby bottles (1 if nursing, 4-8 if bottle-feeding)

_____ formula (2-week supply if bottle-feeding)

Next to the items you have checked, list possible economical sources for obtaining that item. Thank God for His provision for your growing family.

Hopes and Dreams

My dreams for my child's future include _____

_____

_____

My dreams for my spouse's future include _____

_____

_____

My dreams for my own future include _____

_____

_____

Notes

(List any questions you have concerning insurance coverage, doctor/hospital bills, and so on.)

4

Is Your Older Child Ready for a Baby?

Being ready to become parents is one thing. Preparing an older child for a new baby is quite another. How can you tell if he or she is capable of being a good sibling?

In today's medical climate, it is quite possible to plan the minimal time between children. Many variables exist, however, that make exact spacing impossible. A friend of mine has four children, two of them only 18 months apart. She told me one day, "Our family was planned. We wanted four children. But it just wasn't *well* planned." Meeting the needs of three preschoolers and a kindergartner will exhaust any parent!

I'm sure I'll never forget the look on 18-month-old Charlie's face when he first saw his baby sister in his own crib. He evidenced curiosity, confusion, and great sadness over this one who had robbed him of his babyhood. He had to become a big brother too soon.

By contrast, Joy, who was four when her brother arrived, fit smoothly into her role of big sister and Mom's helper. She and her brother were not really close to each other early on, however. When he was learning to walk, she was off to school and into her own world. Later in life they spanned the age difference with a close friendship.

Most developmental psychologists believe three years between children is ideal. The older child will have built the solid foundation of trust that will weather the demands for consistent, intensive care and response by parents to the needs of the new baby. He or she will be through the mutually difficult and demanding periods of the twos. The child will have weathered most of that early ambivalence and pain of separation from the parents. He or she will be quite able to feed himself or herself, can dress sometimes, and probably will be out of diapers. By three, the child will be ready to entertain himself or herself for extended periods of time and hopefully will have mastered a degree of obedience and helpfulness.

Three-year-olds are usually secure enough to feel only minimal jealousy. They can, in fact, put their own parenting instincts to use in watching and interacting with the baby—under your careful supervision, of course.

If you are in the fortunate category who have time to evaluate your older child's readiness for a new baby, here are some guidelines to help you.

Ability to Live Within Boundaries

If your older child is unwilling to accept your required noes and yeses, having a new baby could be a disaster. Imagine a big brother who might harm the baby out of jealousy or who refuses to stay out of baby's room while the baby is sleeping. Maybe he literally devastates the kitchen while you are nursing the baby. Probably you know families in which such disasters occur even without the distraction of a new baby's needs.

If your child has not learned to bend his or her will or postpone his or her desires for at least a short time, adding a baby to this child's life and yours will be a challenge. Correcting this trait is important to successful child rearing, so let me give you a few pointers. Later books will add more details.

1. Explain that there are some new policies to learn. Make these few clearly stated and consistently enforced. An example is this: "Jane, it's time for bed. As soon as the timer rings, you must put away your toys, and I'll help you get ready for bed."

2. Be prepared to follow through if Jane delays or refuses. That timer will remind you. Take Jane lovingly and firmly by the hand, or firmly in your arms if she kicks and screams, as the case may be. Help her through whatever her bedtime routine may be. Then, firmly and as lovingly as possible, put her to bed.

3. Stay with this child if need be to keep her in bed until she understands that she must follow the rule.

Once you establish a healthy respect for your guidance and parental authority in one area of life, you will find other issues become a little bit easier. If you relent and even once give the power back to a headstrong child like Jane, it will be even more difficult to win the next round.

This procedure will not damage your child's personality unless you are downright mean and abusive. There has been a long-term philosophy in our Western culture that gives undue power to children. They do not have the wisdom or experience to know how to handle such power. You must be kind, clear thinking, and in good control of your own feelings in order to prevent your child from taking excessive authority. You need to keep your child's self-respect and to encourage smart, simple choices. But you must establish protective boundaries within which your child can safely function as a child, not as a boss of the family.

Ability to Exhibit Self-control

Haley, a sparkly, energetic three-year-old, was noted for her temper fits. When she could not quickly get her way, she would grab the nearest object, brandishing it like a sword. It could hit her mother's body or knock over any fragile item within the object's reach. She would not stop her rampage even if it meant hurting baby brother.

Her parents learned to grasp Haley securely in their arms whenever she started her explosions. They restrained her firmly, with tough love, until she stopped thrashing about and regained her own control. It took three eternally long weeks to stop Haley's tornadic violence. Imagine the delight both she and her parents enjoyed when that war for self-control was won.

You can see how wise it is to think and plan for even a second or third child. It makes you evaluate your entire family and enables you to correct deficiencies that needed mending anyway.

Ability to Take Some Care of Self

Few children by age three can take total care of themselves. They need a parent to assist, remind, and praise them in their daily routines. The more an older child can do, however, the easier it is on the parents of a new baby.

You must know both your child and yourself well. Each parent has an unconscious philosophy about parenting. Some feel they are great parents if they are totally self-sacrificing and do everything for their children. They believe children must always be happy. Furthermore, for them, happy means carefree. They keep their kids close to them, even dependent.

These parents fail to realize they must balance their caretaking with an increase in the child's independence. A parent must *rarely* do anything for his or her child that the child is capable of doing. The ultimate goal of wise parents is to prepare their child for release into the world as a young adult who is capable of providing for himself or herself, being productive, and willing to help care for those who may not be able to care for themselves. The foundation for building to that goal begins in childhood. Planning thoughtfully for a new baby will help you improve your parenting skills for older children as well.

Teach your older child to dress himself or herself. Choose garments that go on and pull off fairly easily, and be there to assist if he or she gets stuck in a T-shirt. Help the child learn not only to use the toilet but also to flush it; to put toys and books into their proper places; to run occasional errands for you; and to accept the praise and appreciation you will give. Imagine how much more enjoyment all of you will experience when the new baby arrives. You will be building sound self-esteem in your child through this process as well.

Some Compassion for Others

Baby Bryan was only nine months old when I saw an amazing demonstration of empathy. His mother had endured a very trying experience, and as she related the story, she could not stop the tears that dripped onto his romper. In amazement he peered up into his mother's sad face. Then he placed his chubby hands gently on her cheeks and kissed her. I had not realized so young a child could so empathically react to another's pain with such comfort. I realized that this special mom had often kissed away Bryan's tears.

Copy this child's tender example. Give to your own child and to each other the honor of seeing, caring about, and responding to them with compassion. Then consider how satisfying it will be when your older child cares about the baby's cries instead of being the one who caused the pain.

In spite of the most perfect teaching you may provide, your older child will experience periods of jealousy and may well wish the baby would go away. Later books in this series will go into depth about coping with this. You need to know only that this is normal and that it will pass. You will fare better, of course, if you know that jealousy is dispelled in the sunlight of sound security. Give a bit of babying to your older child, lots of reassurance about having plenty of love to go around, and the benefits of sincerity. Sibling rivalry of this sort will pass.

Passing On Equipment

Usually an older child can be moved into a youth bed, freeing up the baby bed for the new family member. But if this transfer is not accomplished wisely, the toddler may feel displaced, hurt, and angry.

Since time moves more slowly for children than for adults, you could make the change only a few months before the arrival date of the baby. One mom I know set up the youth bed close to her son's baby bed. She fitted it with colorful sheets and appealing toys. She explained that he was becoming a really big boy and that this was his big-boy bed. Equally important, she told him that she knew he often felt like a little boy and that it was OK to be little. She asked him to choose the time when he felt like trying out the new bed.

In only a few weeks he was taking naps in the new big bed. Soon he was ignoring the crib and had adopted the big bed completely. The crib was put away to await the arrival of the baby. When that time came, Mother told stories to big brother about his baby days and how he had slept in the little bed. Some children would have asked to try it out again. That's OK, because the older child will quickly find it to be uncomfortable and spontaneously return to his or her own place. Self-discoveries are usually much more effective than parent-child power struggles. I firmly believe in parents' setting boundaries and enforcing them consistently. As your child grows, however, you will find that allowing some space to try out both new and old experiences can be a great teaching method.

Family policies have such a multitude of benefits. By passing on equipment, you are economizing. You are teaching older children the benefits of growing up and of sharing, and the fun of memories of their early days. As the baby grows, he or she may also benefit from discovering that big brother once was little as he or she is and that he even slept in his or her little bed—a useful tool for bonding siblings.

If your older child is very young and not yet able to talk, your task is harder. In fact, if there is less than two years between them, you may have to invest in a second baby bed. Or you may borrow one for the few months you'll need it.

Parents sometimes ask if a newborn and older child can share a bedroom. Of course they can, and sooner or later, perhaps, they should. The early weeks, however, are a time of serious sleep deprivation for most families. Just as you may need to be creative about finding space for baby to be away from your own bed, it makes good sense to keep a newborn away from siblings' beds for a period of a few months. Baby's crying will certainly arouse big siblings, and the nighttime sounds of the older child will disturb most infants. Furthermore, there is some risk of spreading colds by sharing a room. (Of course, this is inevitable with children no matter how much protection you supply.)

Older children accept a new baby best when parents include them in the prenatal events. When parents are natural and have a wholesome attitude, a child will benefit from feeling the baby move about in Mommy's tummy. They may feel where the baby's hands and feet seem to be. One family sang together some cradle songs, with big brother choosing the song. Watching the new baby nurse is quite natural for older children. In fact, it's another chance to crystallize their early experiences as memories. When he was a tiny baby, Danny nursed just as his baby sister does. Mommy loves him all the more because sister sort of reminds her of him.

These and your own creative thinking will help prepare older children for the arrival and early adjustments with the least possible trauma. There will be some tough times in helping any child adjust to a new baby. The changes will be as challenging to adults as they will to youngsters. Understand that this, too, will pass; the newness will vanish in time; and the warmth of healthy family bonding will make it all well worth your efforts.

Expectant Parents' Journal

Chapter 4

Getting in Touch

Ask your children their feelings about the new baby who is coming. Record their answers word for word. _____

_____

_____

_____

What are your feelings about their answers? _____

_____

_____

_____

Are We Ready?

Using the following guidelines, rate your child's readiness for a new baby with a ✓+, ✓, or ✓−. When you've completed the exercise, ask your spouse to do the same.

My older child . . .

You   *Spouse*

_____   _____   can live within boundaries

_____   _____   can exhibit self-control

_____   _____   can take some care of self

_____   _____   has some compassion for others

Develop an action plan to help your child grow in any area where he or she did not receive a ✓+. List the steps of your plan that can be carried out this week:

a.

b.

c.

d.

If you are listening, little one . . .
(Write a message to your unborn child.)

_____

_____

Love Letters

Ask big brother or sister to write a love letter to baby in the space below. (As a parent you may need to write the words as they are dictated from big brother or sister.)

Dear baby,

Prenatal events in which I can include my older child:

Doctor visits

Hospital visits

Planning the nursery

Singing to baby

Feeling baby move

Passing down equipment

Other _____

Checkup!

Special activities my older child and I enjoy doing together:

_____   _____

_____   _____

_____   _____

_____   _____

_____   _____

How often have you shared these activities with your older child during this pregnancy? Schedule specific times this month to enjoy some of them with him or her.

_____

_____

5

Social Issues

Miriam, a new mother of her second child, admitted she was getting serious cabin fever. She loved going out for lunch and was active in numerous volunteer activities. It had been more than four months since she had done any of these activities. Taking care of an energetic preschooler and a hungry infant had consumed her time and left her with little to invest in other things. Her yearning for a bit of her own life to be restored was perfectly normal and necessary for her own sanity.

Erin, on the other hand, vividly recalled that she and her husband had made a vow. They would not allow their children to interfere with their social life. Life, they believed, need not be adapted to children. No indeed—their children would adapt to *their* plans. As succeeding babies arrived, five in all, they dragged them along or left them in the care of the oldest sister. Over time the children became weary of their parents' neglectful attitude, and several developed troubling conduct disorders. They got their parents' attention eventually—in the wrong way.

Somewhere, once again, I urge you to find the healthy balance of some time for yourself, for your marriage, and for your children. Here are some ideas I believe will help you.

How Much Time Do You Need?

There are many factors that determine the social demands on your time. First is your personality and its need for social outlets. Second is your professional life. Some careers come with built-in social events and entertainment of customers or coworkers. Third involves relatives and friends to whom you have various obligations. This may include a range of church activities to which you are faithful.

In order to keep your priorities in the best order, let's reverse the above list and think about church activities. Certainly we agree that it is scripturally sound to keep God first in our lives. But I learned through difficulty that God desires our families, more than the church, to be second to Him. There are some church events that must move down the list. I'm delighted to know many ministers who agree with this concept.

During a particularly hectic period of my family's life, we were involved in developing and building a new church. Driven by exhaustion, I decided to count the evening events that I was committed to attend. To my horror, I realized I was gone 25 nights a month! My husband, the church chairman, was gone even more. No wonder our three young children were fast becoming strangers to us!

Evaluate your obligations before having a child, so you won't be sucked into the vortex of such tornado-like activities. If you are already overcommitted, begin to sort through your obligations. Here are some guidelines that helped restore sanity to my functioning.

1. Are all of these commitments necessary for *me* to do? Could someone else do them as well as I, or even better?

2. Are my church activities connected to my natural talents and spiritual gifts?

3. Am I doing too much in an effort to bolster my own ego? (This is a hard answer to find!)
4. To whom can I go for objective feedback in answering these questions?

Chances are you will be able to cut out from 25 to 50 percent of your church activities without impairing your church's ministry.

Next, consider the demands of relatives. A young couple I know well subtly fell into a pattern of having dinner every Sunday with her parents. If they ever hinted at some other plan, this woman's parents knew exactly how to make her feel guilty. Invariably, the couple gave in but were building massive resentments. Finally, they learned how to negotiate. They agreed to one Sunday dinner a month and an extra day now and then for some special event. Without the resentment, the quality of these family dinners improved immensely.

When they had a child, they could build some of their own family traditions for Sundays. Yet they remained close to the grandparents, who certainly deserved the time with the family too.

Sometimes it is friends who demand too much time and may become possessive. You enjoy them but need more freedom in the relationship. Planning to have a child can give you a perfect out for this problem. Explain to friends that you're starting early to budget your time and to settle down to the new phase of life called parenting. Don't become hostile toward them; maintain a special time when you get together, and don't replace them with other friends. You can expect friends to respect your decision and even to copy your values and priorities.

Social events connected to work are, in some ways, the most difficult to curtail. When your livelihood depends on entertaining customers and your income is essential for your growing family, you may not be able to stop this phase of social life.

It seems to me, however, that corporations are improving their balance sheets by reducing expensive entertaining. You may be able to convince your supervisors to try some other tactic for selling products or services. Another person may relieve you now and then. Be creative and think of new solutions. Once your baby is here, you may be able to find a reliable sitter or grandmother to take care of baby now and then, so consider using business evenings as a date night out together.

How Can You Procure Proper Help?

One of the better moms I know began a search for a reliable child-care person as soon as she began trying to conceive. She advertised, read ads, asked friends, and made phone calls. She interviewed thoroughly and used her exceptionally reliable intuition. She found a just-right person who visited in their home before the baby's birth. This individual became a friend to the parents and was almost a substitute mom after the birth of the child.

Obviously, few families can afford a full-time nanny, or even a part-time housekeeper. But there are several avenues to explore that may help you.

Relatives and friends. Being a four-time grandmother, I can personally say that one of the greatest joys in my life is being with my grandchildren. Equally well, I know I can't always be available, and I trust my children to accept that reality. (Remember the criteria of maturity!) I also understand that not all grandparents feel the way my husband and I do. I have an acquaintance who repeatedly tells her children, "I raised you. I don't want to raise your children!" I feel sorry for her, because she is missing precious moments and memories. Nevertheless, such is reality.

Foster grandparents. Another source of help for those social events you must attend is a set of foster grandparents. There are many grandparents whose children live far from them. They yearn to enjoy the touch and warmth of youngsters. Look around your church and neighborhood for those empty-nest people.

A word of warning here is important. The television and newspapers are full of reports about the catastrophes of child sexual abuse. Frankly, they make it seem common, when in fact it is relatively rare. Spend time with anyone to whom you may ever entrust your child so that you can be certain of your child's safety. If you have any doubts, look for someone else.

Responsible teenagers. Neighborhood or church-affiliated teens are another time-honored source of good child care. Many communities offer special classes for training young people. Youth groups such as Scouts or the YMCA sponsor these. You could probably find such a program in your own community.

Neighborhood trading groups. Several young couples I know have organized themselves into a child care exchange community. They meet to formulate basic rules and appoint a clearinghouse couple to serve as organizers. This duty, of course, changes with some frequency. The basic concept has seemed to work reasonably well. If you feel that you alone can't organize a group like this one, find some partners and do it together.

How Much Time at Home Do You Need?

Many young parents have convinced themselves that anyone can care for a tiny baby. It really won't hurt, they rationalize, if both of them return to work. Certainly, if you must do that to survive, your family can adjust. But careful research from extremely reliable sources has discovered that it takes a great deal of time and love to create in infants the foundational trust that all healthy people need. These studies reveal that the first three years is the vital time for parent-infant bonding to take place. They see the first 18 months as being a critical period, during which a baby needs nearly total care from one of the parents. You can see now why the chapter on economic preparation is so important.

It is my strong recommendation that you plan to spend most of the time nearly every day with your baby for the crucial first year and a half. If you absolutely have to return to work, try to do so only part-time. If at all possible, make that time when your spouse can provide child care.

Studies dating back to the 1950s showed that occasional care of an infant by a third person could be tolerated without serious damage to the bonding of the child with the parents.

Baby-sitters

As early as two or three weeks after a baby is born, you can plan to be away for an evening or a few hours. The crucial factor in how long you, the mother, can be away is whether or not you breast-feed. The preferred nutrition for newborns is mother's milk. For the first three to six weeks, babies need to nurse whenever they are hungry, which can be every two to four hours. Plan to go out during the longer times of sleep, and look for a baby-sitter who has some flexibility. It is remarkable how quickly intuitive and observant mothers figure out a baby's resting and feeding cycle.

I recommend you stay at home most of the time until you know when to be gone without allowing baby to go hungry. Avid breast feeders believe you should not give a bottle to your child if you are nursing. Frankly, I believe it's a common-sense practice to do so. When mothers need to be free now and then (and most do), the ability for fathers or sitters to give a bottle makes everyone happier.

As with foster grandparents, relatives, and friends, thoroughly screen the sitter you will hire. Have such a person familiar to you well before baby is born. New babies bring immeasurable stress for some weeks. You will not be able to interview well or decide objectively whom to hire during that time.

An occasional switch to a new sitter now and then will work unless you have a supersensitive baby. Find someone calm, cautious, and reliable. Your ability to enjoy shopping, visiting, and the necessary social events depends on your confidence in your child's caregiver.

Church Events

Many young couples bring their brand-new babies to church as early as two weeks of age. In preparing to have a child, please think about baby's well-being more than the fun you may anticipate in such a practice.

Prepare your church staff and friends for the fact that neither mother nor child will be in church services for a few weeks. Babies are delightful magnets that attract people in clusters. Every child and adult who knows you will want not only to see the baby but also to hold and kiss him or her. Such people will forget they have a cold. They may not even know they carry virulent strains of bacteria that give them no trouble, but these could create serious infections in a baby.

New babies are gifted by our Creator with remarkable resistance to infections. On the other hand, their skin and mucous membranes are soft and vulnerable to germs. Rather than offend people, I urge you to stay away from crowds until you and your baby are well through the first month of the postpartum period. In planning to have a child, you will need to give up some of your desires for a time. Staying at home for a while will be boring to many moms. But it is a wise decision to make now, well ahead of time.

Church friends, like family members, are usually special people. They will want to visit you and your new infant. Planning ahead can prevent many hurt feelings. Just forewarn them that when you have a child, you'll be very protective. You'll want them to visit one at a time, and only when they're healthy. You have the responsibility to protect the tiny person God will give you. Start thinking early on about how best you can do that.

When Can Baby Go Out?

In a small group of wise and careful people, baby can safely be shown off as soon as Mom feels like going out. Many times baby showers are given after baby is born. Such parties are fun, and people are entitled to see the object of their generosity.

Be sure you observe people carefully. If you notice someone coughing or sneezing, you will want to sit across the room. You may comment, "Beth, hurry and get over that cold so you can come over and hug our baby!" Most friends will watch out for a baby's welfare, but sometimes they forget. Be as courteous as possible, but remember—it's your job, not theirs, to protect your child.

Weather also will guide you about when you can take baby out socially. In fact, you may be able to plan your child's advent for spring or early autumn, or whatever season is mildest in your vicinity. Extreme cold or heat are not well tolerated by babies. With today's technology, of course, that is not a big problem unless you enjoy outdoor events.

Babies are not toys to be tossed about among lots of people, so be careful to plan wisely for a slow start to her or his social debut. While social life is important, its practice can be interrupted for several weeks or months without losing friends. So think ahead, observe other families, and make your plans carefully. By preparing your own minds as well as your friends' ahead of time, you may wisely reenter your social circle.

Expectant Parents' Journal

Chapter 5

Getting in Touch

My *feelings* about the increasing demands on my time and coming changes in schedule are _____

_____

My *thoughts* about the increasing demands on my time and coming changes in schedule are _____

_____

Nurture

List possible child-care providers or baby-sitters, with phone numbers and references.

Name/Organization	Phone Number	References
_____	_____	_____
_____	_____	_____
_____	_____	_____
_____	_____	_____

Questions I want to ask each:

If you are listening, little one . . .
(Write a message to your unborn child.)

_____

_____

For Inspiration

*Behold, children are a gift of the Lord; the fruit
of the womb is a reward* (Ps. 127:3, NASB).

Checkup!

Get out your calendar and jot down every activity you are committed to this month.

Total days I will be out of my house: ____

Total evenings I will be out of my house: ____

This schedule is *(a)* realistic *(b)* unrealistic for a new parent.

Which of these commitments are necessary for *me* to do? (No one else could do them as well.)

Which of these am I doing to bolster my own ego? (Be honest!)

Pray about your schedule, asking God which, if any, activities you should give up. Record them here: _____

_____

_____

I will contact the following people to inform them of my decision: _____

_____

I will take the following steps to ensure I am able to spend as much time as possible with my baby (especially for the first one and a half years): _____

_____

_____

6

Preparing Yourself Psychologically

Some 10 years ago I attended a seminar conducted by Dr. William Glasser. He is a well-known psychiatrist, wise and full of common sense. He has influenced my own thinking. As a result of that day, I have changed some basic concepts. All of us who attended had been taught to help people with psychological problems get in touch with their feelings and express these emotions; it was believed that by "getting their feelings out," they would solve their problems, and life would be fine. And to a degree, that was so.

What we learned from Dr. Glasser, however, added a long-missing ingredient. We saw that painful emotions were nearly always caused by erroneous information and distorted thinking. By learning to acquire accurate information and to take charge of their own thinking and behaviors, these people found that their feelings would automatically change. Furthermore, their attitudes would improve. Personally, I explored these sound concepts, and I found they work well.

Let's apply Dr. Glasser's ideas to your consideration about having a child. Several friends of mine felt overwhelmed by the prospect of raising a child in a world that has become contaminated with toxins and evil. Their anxiety and helplessness created for them a family barren of all the joys and challenges children bring. They chose not to have a child. In their older years they are sadly missing the joy of a grandchild's hugs. They will never hear, as I recently did when my grandson hugged me tightly, "Oh, Grandma, I love you! You smell so good!"

While I feel sad for my friends, I respect their right to choose the course of their own lives. And I respect your right as well. But I challenge you to explore carefully your information and its validity. Look sensibly at your feelings. Are they rooted in sound truth or false, distorted information?

Ginny is a good example of a mother who was trying to decide whether or not to have a third child. Her first two were three years apart, two lovely girls who had a sound sibling relationship. Ginny could not believe that a third child would be able to enter into that already tightly established bonding. You see, Ginny had grown up with two older siblings who had effectively crowded her out. She had felt lonely and understandably hurt by their exclusion of her for most of her childhood.

Ginny and I thought carefully about the facts. She and her husband were very different from her parents. For example, they involved themselves more in activities and were highly sensitive to their children's feelings. They did not tolerate hurtful behaviors and knew how to encourage healthy interaction between them. In fact, the majority of circumstances in this family were very different from those in her childhood.

It was fascinating to observe Ginny's facial expression as we talked. The tense muscles relaxed, a slow smile spread broadly, and the merry twinkle returned to her eyes. Gone was her anxiety. She no longer felt helpless, knowing she had the tools for building a healthy relation-ship among as many or as few children as she and her husband chose.

Silly Myths

I was blessed to grow up in a huge extended family. As simple an event as Sunday dinner provided an excuse to get together with various uncles, aunts, and cousins. Then, as now, the men tended to congregate in one area and women in another. I rarely heard the topics that occu-pied men talk, though it usually had to do with planting crops, the latest hailstorm's damage, or chronically rotten prices.

Women, on the other hand, discussed babies, who was expecting one and when, and how many children that family already had. Then, in hushed tones and disguised words, they would talk about labor and delivery. I recall feeling uneasy and would run off to play. But I grew up thinking that the birth of a child was a torturous process that could be fatal. Tragically enough, that once was so. But even in these days I suspect many a young wife has deferred having a child or has chosen to never have one because of fear based on false information.

My youngest daughter recently gave birth to her third child. She insists she felt not one pain, had no incision or trauma, and her baby arrived within four hours of the on-set of labor. Recent medical advances have provided anes-thesia that allows moms to be wide-awake and aware of every development but free of pain with no risks to baby's safety. This is one more bit of information that can set your mind at rest as you contemplate whether or not to have a child.

Reactive Parenting

Over some four decades of working with families, I have learned a profoundly significant truth. Most parents raise their children *reactively*. By that I mean they go through each day somewhat blindly. If baby cries, they try to find out what he or she wants and usually end up feeding him or her. If baby is older, they'll look around to see who or what hurt him or her. They then try to take care of the offender. Baby *acts* a certain way, so Mom or Dad *re*acts accordingly. This is not all bad. It relies on good parenting instincts and baby's innate expression of need or pain. There are, however, some risks with this kind of parenting:

1. *Parents' instincts can go awry.* A dad, for example, may instinctively feel that a boy should not cry. I heard of a father who believed this so strongly that when his son was only three months old, he spanked him when he cried. Logic should have taught this man that crying is a baby's only God-given language. By that alone could his son say, "I'm wet, hungry, and lonely!" Dad's instincts were warped by misinformation and crooked thinking.

2. *Mom's instincts are almost certain to vary from Dad's in some areas of life.* When these differences are quite distinct, they create a climate for manipulating. Children learn amazingly early which parent is the softer-easier one, the stronger-safer one, or the harsher-frightening one. They gravitate early on to safety, later on to permissiveness.

3. *Babies' needs and actions change with time and vary according to inborn, temperamental traits.* Unless parents understand these differences, their instincts alone will misguide them. In infancy, for example, a baby's needs are extremely fundamental —food, warmth, rocking, and physical comfort. Later on, a toddler must have language, teaching, and protection through gentle logic, consistency, and parental presence.

Proactive Parenting

Proactive parenting requires thinking, planning, and goal setting. Are you good at these functions? If not, now is the time to master them. Find some extended time together and discuss the issues you each feel to be vital to excellent child rearing.

1. *Goals.* What kind of child do you want yours to become? If you want your child to be kind and tenderhearted, treat him or her gently but firmly so he or she will be safe enough to care about others. Require your child to show respect by modeling and verbally teaching respect. When your child fails to be respectful, stop the misbehavior, correct him or her, continue to love him or her, and your child will finally master it.

   Whatever your goals for yourselves as parents as well as for your child, make them clear, pinpoint how to reach them, and follow through. Such techniques do not happen automatically. Think *now* about these issues.

2. *Unanimity.* In the best families, parents come to basic agreement on most issues. Certainly they disagree here and there, but they are willing to discuss, negotiate, and arrive at harmonious conclusions. This quality demands clear thinking, open expression, the ability to honestly consider every aspect of any situation, and the determination to avoid power struggles—the futile fights to get *my* way.

3. *Plans.* To have a specific plan in mind regarding training children is of utmost importance. What is amazing to me is that reactive parenting works as well as it does.

   Trishia was one of my most delightful case studies. She had sparkling brown eyes and curly blond hair that bounced with her energetic motion. The problem was that she also had an explosive temper that was fast becoming an embarrassment to her and her parents as she grew older. The parents had "tried everything," a tip-off to me that the consistency such a child needs was missing.

Together we came to see clearly the pattern of Trishia's outbursts and formulated a workable plan of action. When both parents employed that plan every time the tantrums exploded, they miraculously decreased and stopped. I shall not forget that mother's words: "Once I knew what to do, the rest became easy."

4. *Follow-through.* No matter how lofty your goals, how clear your plans, nor how close your teamwork, they are useless unless you follow through. *Just do it!*

Now is the time, before you have any children—or even if you do—to become proactive. Surely you can see the benefits. Of course it takes thought, information gathering, and commitment. It will even feel risky to try out ideas that are different from the ones familiar to you. But by starting now, you have time to discuss them with others to test their logic. You may even encourage your friends who have children to try them and observe the results.

Empathy

The ability to feel with others but not to fall into despair with them is a blessed quality. We tend to go to certain extremes with those who experience distress. Either we identify with them so much that we become enveloped in their pain, or we see them as weak and draw away from them. In either case, it's difficult to help them.

Good psychological functioning finds the balance between these extremes. One of my favorite Bible verses is Ps. 103:13: "As a father pities his children, so the LORD pities those who fear Him" (NKJV). My interpretation of a good father's pity is not that he rescues them from their failures and disappointment, but that he tenderly guides and encourages his children through the difficulties. Thus the children learn and grow.

Now is the time to understand this concept and to practice empathizing with others.

Understanding

Both empathy and proactive parenting will be enhanced by understanding others. One of our most common mistakes is to believe others are like we are. In some very basic ways there is truth to that. But there are some treacherous pitfalls as well.

I have struggled throughout life to be scrupulously honest. Because of that belief I have been tricked and conned in many ways. I have lost thousands of dollars by naively believing people would repay loans. And several cherished books are missing from my shelves because friends have failed to return them.

It is vital to know how to assess other people objectively if you are to be a wise parent. Millie came home from school frequently with tales of woe about other children being mean to her. Her mother sympathized and angrily talked about the teacher and other parents. A major battle was launched to protect poor Millie! The teacher, however, after careful observation found only the usual peer competition. She described Millie as a successful student, well liked most of the time, with only the usual transient disagreements.

The truth was, Mom had suffered some genuine abuse from classmates when she grew up. Millie's relatively minor conflicts seemed like carbon copies of her remembered pain. She could not understand Millie accurately because she was too close, overidentifying with her.

So learn to step back emotionally, far enough to be objective. See others and their situations simply and clearly, separate from you and your experiences. In other words, balance empathy with objective logic, and you will reach healthy understanding. Practice this skill with each other, and you will be better prepared to practice blue-ribbon parenting.

Understanding requires these ingredients:

1. *Accurate information about an event or a behavior.* Such information is acquired by unbiased thinking, careful observation, and sometimes questioning another person.

2. *Self-awareness, especially regarding strong emotions you experience.* Ask yourself what feeling you have. Name it accurately. Try to discover why you have that specific emotion in a given situation. Try to recall when you first experienced that feeling, and separate that event from the here and now. This mental exercise will enable you to be free to cope objectively with a current situation.

3. *Sensitivity to the other person's feelings and needs.* With young children this step is most important. Many annoying habits and problems of children emanate from their deep inner needs. They do not have the words to use for asking, so they act out those feelings. Philip felt lonely and abandoned when his baby sister required too much of Mom's energy. He reverted to thumb-sucking and wetting his pants in an effort to regain Mother for himself. Punishing him for "misbehaving" could only have exaggerated his fears. Understanding his symptoms enabled Mom to find time to cuddle and baby Phil until he regained his certainty that he was still important. Mom still loved him too!

Cultivate the skill of achieving understanding. You see, psychology is not weird or mystical. It is thinking, planning, and learning to live with love and logic.

Expectant Parents' Journal

Chapter 6

Getting in Touch

My *feelings* about my own childhood are _____

_____

My *thoughts* about my own childhood are _____

_____

Self-test

My primary fear about raising a child is _____

_____

This fear started when _____

_____

Is this fear rooted in truth or in erroneous information? _____

_____

Three things I can do to combat this fear:

a.

b.

c.

Look up the following scriptures. Choose one to memorize this week, and write it below.

Ps. 34:4   Isa. 41:10

1 John 4:18   Ps. 23
Prov. 31:30   Ps. 46:1-3

_____

_____

_____

_____

If you are listening, little one . . .
(Write a message to your unborn child.)

_____

_____

For Inspiration

*May your father and mother be glad; may she who
gave you birth rejoice!* (Prov. 23:25).

Checkup!

Proactive Parenting

Think about the kind of person you want your unborn child to become. List 10 character traits (honesty, compassion, and so on) that you want to develop in him or her. Ask your spouse to do the same.

You   *Spouse*

_____   _____

_____   _____

_____   _____

_____   _____

_____   _____

_____   _____

_____   _____

_____   _____

_____   _____

_____   _____

Talk about each of these with your spouse. Define them and brainstorm practical ways to build them into your child's life.

Case Study

Your three-year-old, Tricia, is fast developing an explosive temper. One Saturday afternoon you, your spouse, and Tricia are on your way to an important social engagement. You stop at a store to pick up a last-minute gift. Tricia spies a doll she wants—a doll she doesn't need and one you can't afford to buy. You quietly say no, but Tricia throws herself on the floor, kicking and screaming. What will you do? Ask your spouse what he or she would do. Dialogue about the similarities and differences in your approach to this hypothetical situation.

Notes

(Rewrite in your own words the scripture you chose to memorize in the Self-test section.)

7

Are Your Emotions an Asset or a Liability?

More years ago than I like to count, I was a pediatrician. For more than eight years I examined newborn babies—hundreds of them. As soon as possible after their traumatic birth process, I undressed them, listened to their breathing and heartbeats, checked their reflexes, measured them carefully, and looked in every orifice in order to be sure they were healthy. Fortunately, the great majority of them were quite normal.

In the process of all of this exploring I discovered newborns demonstrated only two basic emotions. To my chagrin these were *anger* and *fear*. While babies elicit deeply loving, tender emotions from adults, especially parents, at birth they do not show love by any demonstrable evidence. Apparently God the Creator made it necessary for infants to learn love from those to whom He entrusts them.

In infants, anger, the emotion I once dreaded, is sometimes prompted by experiencing pain. When we had to prick that tender skin in order to draw a few drops of blood for necessary tests, babies all reacted identically.

They would let out a howl that was undeniably an expression of rage. Their fists clenched, and their feet, legs, hands, and arms would draw close to their bodies. They usually thrashed about a bit, the cries were relentless, and their eyes would squeeze tightly shut.

Fear, by contrast, was seen when I made a sudden, loud noise near the baby's ear, or if I jolted the crib. In such a case, the baby's eyes opened wide as if in surprise. The arms and legs extended, and often the body would tremble. There was usually a shrill cry that sounded quite different from the cry of rage. After this initial response, the baby who was startled would close his or her eyes, clench those hands into fists, and draw the arms and legs in toward the body.

My interpretation of these two inborn emotions is that they are implanted by the Heavenly Father for His express purposes. Sin certainly distorts both their meaning and their expression, but let's try to understand them.

Were human beings not given the energy of the anger response to pain, many would die. Pain initiates a self-protective instinct that prompts us to flee or fight to save our very lives. People with leprosy demonstrate the value of pain and withdrawal clearly. Their disease destroys the pain neurons in various parts of their bodies. They therefore cannot feel extreme heat, cold, or pressure and are unaware of the damage these cause to tissues. Over time, they actually lose parts of their bodies because of those destructive forces and their bodies' numbness.

So when you see an infant crying in anger, or later fighting off toddler foes, be grateful for this God-given self-protective aggression. Later on, anger is prompted by emotional pain even more than physical. It is a sign of a body and mind that are sensitive to pain and can learn to protect the person. Certainly that aggression must be brought under God's control so it won't become even more hurtful than the "attacker." But do see the good in it, as well as the potential for evil in inborn aggression. I am no longer afraid of most anger.

Fear, in turn, has its own level of usefulness. The physical fears we identify in babies are of falling and of loud noises. Once again you can see that this emotion of fear is God-given. It helps us avoid danger and teaches us to understand that loud noises can signal the approach of harm. The anger instinct prepares us to run or fight. The fear with which we are born gives us caution and the sense to avoid the danger.

There are also two kinds of psychological fear: the fear of abandonment and the fear of engulfment. So now you know why babies cry when they are left alone too long or when they are held too tightly for too long.

Perhaps you can already perceive the implications of these facts about emotions in your own adult life. From the simple, instinctive rage born of the various experiences of pain of the new baby evolve all the aggressive emotions of our adult lives. Irritation and frustration bounce out of our mouths when daily frictions from others hamper our progress or hurt our feelings. Gossip against us causes an instinctive urge to get even. A coworker's manipulation to crowd us out of our rightful promotion can result in feelings of helpless rage or hurtful retaliation.

In your marriage, anger in its various forms can become common when you allow misunderstandings to result in unresolved emotional pain. No wonder all too many marriages are lived out in cycles of abuse or even in constantly recurring hurts. You cannot be a safe parent, obviously, unless you have learned to control your emotions.

In order to heal and prevent this pain, you must be sensitive to both your own feelings and those of others. In fact, you cannot be adequate parents until you have mastered this capability. Furthermore, you must learn to respond, not to the rage you hear, but to that pain you know lies beneath it. Soothing the pain dissolves the rage.

Similarly, to cope with fear, you must understand its lifesaving intent. Without caution, children as well as adults are at extreme risk. Cautious people are not cowards—they are wise. I see people who are in despair, really not wanting to live, who expose themselves to needless danger, unconsciously wishing to die. Caution could save their lives. On the other hand, people may become so afraid that they move to the extreme of caution, which is anxiety or even panic.

Now you must see once again the vital necessity of balance. The self-protective function of anger can explode into the counterattack of assault on another. All of us have experienced such attacks verbally, and some of us have felt the pain of physical abuse as well. Inborn anger, when uncontrolled and intense, can result in crimes of passion instead of simply taking care of oneself.

Fear, when it becomes a phobia, can imprison people for years in a single room of their own homes. Caution, like anger, can become so magnified that it cripples lives.

Anthony is an example of the intertwining of fear and anger. His situation clearly portrays the crucial significance of love. When Anthony was two, he became a daily revelation of the interplay of anger and fear. If he fell, scraping his knee, he refused to allow anyone to touch it, courageously marching about stiff-legged. He would not allow the tears of pain to flow nor acknowledge his need of his mother's ministrations. He would be independent and take care of himself, thank you!

Anthony's mother had to work during the week, but weekends were their time for play and closeness. One Saturday Mommy had to work overtime, leaving him to the care of his doting grandmother. His grandmother drove some distance, eagerly anticipating an entire half day with him. They were good buddies.

Not long after Mommy left, however, Anthony began to act angry. He flounced about, refusing to play. He would not let Grandma hold him, read to him, or comfort him. Soon he stomped off, out of sight. Grandma assumed he would return in a bit with his usual smiles and effervescence. After considerable time elapsed, however, she went in search of him. She was surprised to see him quietly standing by the window in his bedroom. He looked angrily out at the empty driveway below. She was even more surprised when he saw her peering around the doorframe at him and yelled at her, "Grandma, you get outta my house!"

Anger always begets anger, and Grandma felt very much like yelling back at this seemingly rude behavior. How should she react?

Fortunately, this lady had learned not to *react*, but to be *pro*active. Gently she responded, "Anthony, now I understand why you wouldn't come to me and play with me. You really want Mommy, and she's gone! If I were *out* of your house, Mommy would be *in* your house to love you. You miss her." The miracle of Grandma's wisdom, interpretation, and patience worked. Anthony could finally run to her welcoming arms. The tears of his longing were released, and the healing was soon complete.

Anger became Anthony's cover-up for his fear about Mommy's absence and his yearning for her to be there. What if Grandma had scolded him for his rudeness instead of reaching through it to the thorn prick of his underlying longing and anxiety? His own anger was already outweighing his fear. Had she poured her understandable anger on top of Anthony's, it could easily have broken his little spirit, convincing him that he was totally abandoned.

This is in truth what I believe happens to many little children. Once that tender spirit is wounded, it takes a long time to heal, and sometimes it never does. This accounts for many of the calloused, abusive kids who are worrisome in our culture.

How does all of this apply to preparing for parenthood? First of all, it can greatly enhance the building of a strong marriage. If you've already read the first book of this series, *Marriage: First Things First,* you know how vital that solid foundation of a healthy family is.

You may very well see the shadow of little Anthony in your spouse's occasional rage. If you probe carefully through each other's anger to the quivering area of pain beneath, you will avoid most of the harmful exchanges of anger in your home. Imagine how grateful you will feel when your spouse responds to your occasional angry outbursts with understanding and comfort like Anthony's grandmother. You would be so grateful and feel so comforted that you would love your spouse through many another fault.

You may never have experienced this type of healing response to pain and anger. And you may understandably believe that you could never do that. Let me assure you—you can. The first time you try, you will fumble a bit, and you will feel awkward and embarrassed. Just keep doing it. Practice by dialoguing with yourself in a mirror. Or try writing out a script on some paper. Ask a friend to role-play with you. Be creative, but do not settle for the continued practice of living and interacting in anger.

Some years ago the title of a paperback book leaped out at me from the bookstore shelf. It yelled, *Love Is Letting Go of Fear.* I did not purchase the book, but its title teaches a valid lesson that echoes in my memory. The Bible states the same truth with its simple authority: "There is no fear in love; but perfect love casts out fear, because fear involves torment" (1 John 4:18, NKJV).

When you and your spouse master the art of recognizing and expressing your anger and fear in appropriate and healthy ways, you will be ready to train and discipline a child. You will not need to worry about ever abusing him or her.

You will recall reading at the beginning of this chapter that babies are born with the primal emotions of only fear and anger. Then how do we find love? Anthony's grandma's love served as a secure fulcrum on which his natural seesaw of fear and anger could find a balance. It offered him the safe climate in which neither was needed in that event.

Let's think together about finding and cultivating the abundance of safe, joyful living that only love can provide. One of the shortest Bible verses most succinctly defines love. "He who does not love does not know God, for God is love" (1 John 4:8, NKJV).

"You don't wanna hear the words I think when I'm mad!" These were the words of Connie, just 11 years old. She was well mannered, neatly groomed, with bright eyes and a ready smile. She and her family were active in church and practiced Christian values faithfully. Most kids think angry thoughts, so I was certain I could help her learn to deal with her "mad" words.

It was a surprise to me, then, when only a few days later Connie's pressure cooker of rage exploded. She threatened to hurt her parents, tried to run away, and literally tore up the house before she regained control.

In spite of this family's excellent appearance and their honest values, they had occasionally allowed anger to rule their interactions. These occasions recurred with enough frequency to teach Connie how to be angry. When her emotional dam burst, the stored-up fury of 11 years poured forth. Eventually she learned to control her rage and express it constructively through words.

It is extremely important that parents practice healthy

emotional expression and require that of their children. Here are three steps that will make any feeling a useful force instead of a destructive power.

1. *Name the feeling.* Strong feelings can actually control people, causing devastation around them. When you think about your anger even enough to name it accurately, you are gaining control over that emotion.

2. *Explain the feeling.* As you think about what aroused the feeling, you're gaining even more wise control over it. Furthermore, if you take time, you can recall a long trail of habits and events that began in your early life that resemble this episode. You can learn to separate those old memories from the present event, coping much more logically with the here and now.

3. *Decide what you can do about this event.* Most angry people tell the other person off. Few of us think at such times about our own power. What a destructive reversal that practice is! In most cases we can't make another person do a given thing. But we can choose to walk away until we regain control, to silently count to 10, or to do whatever it takes to calm down, think clearly, and solve the problem.

You can see quickly that getting ready to have a child demands that your emotional control system be in excellent shape. Let me explain what that control system really is. Many Christians try to hide all their negative feelings. Not only does that not work, but also it allows emotions to build up until, as with Connie, they explode. And all too often such outbursts occur at the worst time and in places that leave us with embarrassment or even broken relationships.

Repression

The worst thing to do with any emotion or memory is to repress it. Repression means that you block it from your conscious mind. That, of course, frees you from the pain such emotions cause, but it leaves their impact imprinted deep inside. When a new occasion arises, resembling the old one, even more pain will reoccur.

If you have a child, he or she is likely to go through many experiences in life similar to yours. Chances are that when they occur, you will overreact to your child's problems, mishandling them somewhat, because of your old, buried emotions.

Suppression

This practice involves hiding your feelings so others won't see them. You may, for example, believe it's a lack of faith to feel sad or depressed. Or you have been taught that anger is always bad. So you may mask your face, control your voice, and believe you are fooling those around you. These maneuvers rarely work. In fact, people will recognize that something is wrong, and they may imagine it to be worse than it actually is.

Children are incredibly attuned to parents' emotions. Be well assured that you can never fool them. To be ready for a child, then, requires you to be open, as well as honest, about your feelings.

Expression

Expressing feelings appropriately, honestly, and yet with control is the wisest way of dealing with them. Years ago, robbers broke into our home and helped themselves to many of our most cherished, sentimental items—things that were entwined with special events and celebrations in our family. I felt horror, terror, rage, and a useless desire for revenge. Fortunately, my family and friends were equally outraged. They willingly listened as I poured out these intense emotions over and over. After a remarkably short time, I began to feel better. The intensity of my negative emotions subsided, and at last I became quite matter-of-fact about the whole invasion.

On many occasions of crisis a similar truth has emerged. Those who talk about their pain and trauma recover from the tragedy significantly faster and more completely than those who hide their emotions.

The important aspect of expressing feelings, however, lies in doing so appropriately. To express anger in uncontrolled rage is highly damaging. Not to express it at all is hurtful in a different way, but to use the simple steps described above is constructive, air clearing, and problem solving.

If the feeling is sadness, worry, love, or excitement, the formula works uniformly: Here's how I feel. Here's why. Here's what I will do about both the feeling and the reason. Problem solved!

Whether or not you decide to have a child, recognizing and properly expressing your feelings are ingredients of a worthwhile lifestyle. By beginning today, you can master this skill and enrich your relationships.

Jesus wept over the city of Jerusalem and the inhabitants who rejected Him. He railed at the hypocrisy of the dishonest Pharisees. He cleansed the holy Temple in an absolute rage. His example of emotional honesty is one to explore and follow carefully.

Expectant Parents' Journal

Chapter 7

Getting in Touch

My *feelings* about Dr. Ketterman's statement that infants experience only two basic emotions (fear and anger) are _____

_____

_____

My *thoughts* about this statement are _____

_____

_____

Read and Review

List the reasons Dr. Ketterman gives for citing anger and fear as God-given emotions:

Anger: _____

_____

Fear: _____

_____

Before reading this chapter, did you think of anger and fear as God-given emotions? Why or why not? _____

_____

Beneath rage lies _____. Soothing the pain dissolves the _____.

Reread the story about Anthony. What insights did you gain from the story? Write about a time when you have seen anger wound someone's spirit.

_____

_____

_____

_____

_____

_____

_____

If you are listening, little one . . .

(Write a message to your unborn child.)

_____

_____

For Inspiration

For his anger lasts only a moment, but his favor lasts a lifetime; weeping may remain for a night, but rejoicing comes in the morning (Ps. 30:5).

Checkup!

Is your emotional control system in excellent shape? Do you repress, suppress, or express the way you feel?

Recall the last time you felt angry. Evaluate your responses, using the text to refresh your memory if you need it.

Did you *name the feeling?*

_____

_____

_____

Did you *explain the feeling?*

_____

_____

_____

Did you *consciously decide what to do about the event?*

_____

_____

_____

Remembering Dr. Ketterman's advice about accepting constructive criticism, ask your spouse how he or she perceives your emotional control. (Remember, the emotional health of your child depends largely on your ability to provide an emotionally stable environment.)

Notes
(Write a prayer asking God to empower you to give an emotionally healthful environment to your baby.)

8

What If You Can't Have a Child?

After a lingering illness, Tina's mother had died. We sat talking softly of her grief and the legacy of love and wisdom her mother had left. Somewhat abruptly, my friend spoke of her strong wish for a child of her own. She had been married several years and had not thought much about having a child. Losing her mother, however, had helped her realize the treasure of intimacy the two of them had enjoyed. Yes, she decided, it was time now, in her early 30s, to start her own family. She and Charles would pass on the heritage her parents had given her.

In the months and years that followed, this couple tried every remedy they could find for the infertility they discovered. Modern medicine has many techniques for overcoming a problem like theirs. But many thousands of dollars and months of trying resulted in not one conception. They grieved another death—that of a lost dream of happy children and a warm, loving family such children would complete.

Once their grief had healed, they decided to adopt children, and they were able to do so. They now have a delightful household, full of activity, laughter, and a great appreciation for the love they almost missed.

Perhaps you, too, have already tried to conceive a child without success. You may be worried about the possibility of infertility. What if you can't have children?

Patience

First of all, remember that many couples try to conceive a child for a year or more before they finally succeed. Your doctor can instruct you about detecting the most likely time of the month for ovulation to occur. The body temperature and degree of acidity or alkalinity of the vagina will change at that time. Some doctors believe that sexual abstinence for several days before this period of time can make for a higher sperm count and a greater possibility of conception.

Avoid becoming overly anxious. Anxiety and stress may inhibit conception. Keep your lovemaking relaxed and pleasurable. Wives, after sexual intercourse, lie flat on your back and elevate your hips on a pillow. This will help insure that the semen reaches the fallopian tubes, where most conception takes place.

Medication

If the above measures fail, by all means see a specialist in fertility problems. He or she can test both spouses to determine if there are correctable measures to be taken. It is quite common to give women medication to increase ovulation and help achieve pregnancy. The best known is called Clomid, which has a fairly high success rate in enabling women to become pregnant. It does have an interesting side effect. It often results in multiple eggs being released from the ovaries, so the likelihood of twins (or more) is quite high. Occasionally medication can increase the number and healthy motility of the husband's sperm. The field of medicine is not as helpful in the case of infertile men as in women. Do be sure that neither of you blames the other, and by all means avoid and/or discard any guilt you may feel about your infertility. It's not your fault, and it certainly does not mean you fail to be truly masculine or feminine.

The Gift Program

Modern medical science has developed amazing, almost frightening, technology. As you may know, ova (the mother's eggs) can be removed from the ovaries and placed into a special fluid, where they can be fertilized by the husband's own sperm or those of a donor. These fertilized eggs will grow for a time in the laboratory until the optimum time is reached for implantation in the wife's uterus.

Several of these fertile eggs are carefully placed in the mother's womb—planted in the vascular lining. There, if they attach, they will grow into healthy babies. Once again, it is likely that more than one will implant, so multiple births are not uncommon.

No matter how hard you and your doctor try, however, this procedure may not work. It is not as successful as Clomid therapy, and as you may imagine, it is extremely expensive.

Artificial Insemination

This is a procedure in which a woman may be given a vaginal injection of semen from an unknown male donor. Sometimes her own husband's semen may fertilize her ova by this method, or a donor, as above, may be used. Artificial insemination is useful if the husband is infertile. That means he has too few sperm or they lack adequate motility to travel to the ovum and penetrate it. Men who have no such problems may donate their semen to a bank. In the laboratory it is quickly frozen and may be stored for some time. Only one or two professional people know the identity of the donor, so the likelihood of anyone else discovering the biological father's identity is extremely slight.

Once again, this method often fails, and it involves some debatable ideas. Some people believe that using a donor's sperm is the same as committing adultery. In the usual definition of that term, it really is not. If successful, it gives a couple a child who carries at least the mother's genetic makeup.

Another problem with this method lies in the inability of some husbands to accept as his own another man's child. The man who truly loves children and yearns to help his wife become a biological mother can handle this. Over time, if all goes well, many men have been able to forget they were not the biological fathers of these children. They become, in actuality, the real dads who love and devote themselves to their children. Be certain you are absolutely honest with your spouse about your feelings on this sensitive and important decision. Seek good counsel before you seriously consider artificial insemination.

Surrogate Mothers

The reverse of artificial insemination lies in donating a husband's sperm to another woman who may conceive a child by this method, carry it to term, and then give it to the original couple as their own. There have been some notorious cases in which this plan backfired. In a widely publicized case, the biological mother just could not bear to part with the baby at birth. She had carried her for nine months, and she had suffered the pains of labor and delivery for her. And who could blame her for wanting to keep the child she had come to love?

Perhaps there are some boundaries God sets that we must heed. It may be that bearing a child is a blessing not everyone may find. If you are one of those couples, please try to avoid feeling it's because of your being unworthy or unloved by God. We do not have all of the answers to why we are denied some of the desires we crave. I can assure you, however, that if you will allow your grief to heal, you will find other valuable experiences that are possible. Let's look at a few of these.

Adoption

Only this week a family in my church welcomed into their hearts a beautiful baby from across the ocean. That child, and countless like her, had no parents able to care for her. She would have become an institutionalized person, living without the enlivening joy of belonging and being bonded to a special family.

While adopting a baby in America has become difficult, it is still very possible. An adoption from a number of other countries, while costly, is another good option.

Some couples do not feel comfortable with adoption. They fear that a child, not their own, may have genetic defects or some birth injury that would make it difficult for them to accept him or her. Often extended family members have strong feelings against adoption that create conflicts.

Whatever your decision, weigh it well. Try to grow beyond your grief if you cannot conceive your own child. Then decide if you can genuinely, unconditionally accept an adopted child. If not, here are some other suggestions.

Be Foster Parents

There are many children in today's Western world whose parents temporarily cannot care for them. Often such situations involve drug or alcohol abuse. Sometimes single parents lose jobs or suffer prolonged illnesses, or serious abusive situations may fracture the family.

Caring for children from such a family can be a truly redemptive ministry. Often the children are frightened and angry. They may be a real challenge to manage. But what an opportunity they bring with them! Not only may you be a turning point in their lives, but also you could help their parents find new life. Through your faith, the possibilities of God's work are limitless.

Caring for foster children is usually a temporary work. You must do a fine juggling act with your emotions. Temporarily loving and caring for a child reminds you constantly that at some point he or she will be wrenched away from you. Yet if you guard your emotions too closely, you will starve the child's hunger for love and deprive yourself of the joy of parenting for a time. It takes a brave, committed, and mature person to be a really good foster parent. If God leads you to do so, He will miraculously empower you in the task.

Be a Volunteer

In most communities there is a major dearth of volunteers in all areas. Yet through my experiences of more than three decades, volunteers have enriched every program I know about. Children's hospitals often need people to play with chronically ill or handicapped children. Knowing you have touched such children with God's love and yours blesses you as well as the children.

Many single moms or dads struggle heroically against horrible odds. Could you organize a plan for giving a few hours a week of respite for such a parent by taking care of the children? You might develop a creative outreach program for your church that would bless many people.

You may find within your own extended family opportunities to care for children whose parents must work. Such a service carries the risk of not always pleasing the parents, so be careful to establish clear guidelines and boundaries.

Many years ago I challenged families without their own children to team up with other families who were over-stressed. Child care for families in which both parents must work offers immense help to those parents and children. Think how comforted such parents would feel, knowing their kids were loved and secure in your home and care! What an opportunity to live out God's love and to fulfill your own thwarted parenting instincts. Years later I reencountered a couple who had accepted my challenge. For 10 years they had cared for three youngsters in their church. The parents had to work and had been able to survive and become financially stable because of their help.

Choose a Child-Care Career

My oldest sister married later in life and missed the joys of being a mother. I know that grieved her as deeply as being a childless couple hurts you. But she became a teacher. Over the 43 years of her career she loved, corrected, taught, and mothered more children than she could remember.

As a teacher, nurse, child-care person, Sunday School teacher, child therapist, or teacher's aide, you can be an immense blessing to many children. Many of them will try your patience and challenge every skill you have. But you will make a real difference in some of their lives.

If you decide to have children, go all out for it. Pray for clear guidance, and then do whatever you can to follow that plan. If you get to the point, however, of discovering that it may be impossible, remember that life is not over. Look for other avenues to live out the love and tenderness of a good parent. Sublimate that lost wish in giving to others, and you will in turn be blessed more than you can now imagine.

Expectant Parents' Journal

Chapter 8

Getting in Touch

My *feelings* about the possibility of my (or someone I know) not being able to conceive are _____

_____

My *thoughts* about the possibility of my (or someone I know) not being able to conceive are _____

_____

You may have conceived easily. It may have taken several months or years. You may be waiting to conceive or are considering adoption. In the space provided, write a letter to God honestly expressing your feelings about your current situation.

Dear God,

For Inspiration

For you created my inmost being; you knit me together in my mother's womb. I praise you because I am fearfully and wonderfully made (Ps. 139:13-14).

Interact

List the pros and cons of adoption as you see them. Ask your spouse to do the same. Discuss.

	You		Spouse	
Pros	Cons	Pros	Cons
_____	_____	_____	_____
_____	_____	_____	_____
_____	_____	_____	_____
_____	_____	_____	_____

Checkup!

Do you know anyone going through the grieving process because he or she cannot have children?
Write a prayer for that person:

_____

_____

_____

_____

_____

_____

_____

Notes

9

Spiritual Preparation

As Christians, most of us believe that children are a gift from God. They are loaned to us as parents to prepare them to live eternally with Him. Having a child is indeed a gargantuan responsibility in any case. But when we add to those many other aspects of life this immeasurable challenge, you can understand that we must not take lightly the conception of an eternal human life.

How can you prepare yourselves for this awesome responsibility? Here are some ideas to help you.

Accept God's Gifts

"He [God] gave you your life in Christ Jesus, whom God made our wisdom, righteousness, holiness, and ransom from sin, so that it may be as the Bible says: *If you feel proud, feel proud of the Lord*" (1 Cor. 1:30-31, BECK).

The truth of these verses has been validated often in my life's experiences. I have been blessed to share many intimate moments with people who cross my path. Those who accept God's wisdom, forgiveness, and love have the power to be wise parents.

Melvin's parents were a good example of how such power works. It was in his late teens that he began to blossom into a socialite. He loved music, activities, God, and people. But he could not seem to be accountable with his time. On weekend nights he often stayed out beyond his agreed-upon curfew. He was with Christian friends and was often in Bible studies or singing gospel music, but he just didn't come home on time. His mother, however, knew the serious dangers that are especially common late at night, and she worried about her son.

She prayed earnestly for wisdom and then arranged a quiet talk with Melvin. She explained that she trusted him, but she *mis*trusted the world in which he lived. She did not levy unbearable restrictions, which could have created rebellion in her son. But she negotiated an agreement that if he could not be home at the designated time, he would call her to let her know he was OK, where he was, and what time he would be home. Further, he agreed that staying out would not be an excuse for missing work or church.

Because he knew his parents loved him, Melvin readily agreed to this plan. He risked the possibility that his friends might consider him a Mama's boy because he loved her and was willing to reassure her at any cost. He and his mother worked out a somewhat difficult situation because she leaned on God's power and wisdom and because of the love and mutual respect they shared. Throughout parenting, the need for God's gifts is unrelenting.

God is love. When baby Karina cried night after night for 19 months, even her mother's love grew cool. She forgot what it was like to sleep through the night, much less to sleep a bit late in the morning now and then.

Karina's pediatrician examined her carefully and found her to be free from ear infections or any pain that would require her mom's attention at night. Nevertheless, Mom resisted the doctor's recommendation that she allow her child to cry it out for a few nights. She felt it would be cruel to fail to go to a sobbing child no matter how often that occurred.

Eventually, perhaps out of sheer exhaustion, she began to focus on God's *tough* love. He is likely to chasten His children when they err (Heb. 12:5-6, quoting Prov. 3:11-12, NKJV). She realized that tender love was in short supply at 2:30 A.M., so at last she practiced tough love and allowed Karina to cry it out. After 45 minutes of screaming the first night, Karina finally fell asleep. The next night she cried 10 minutes, and the third night she slept like a baby through eight hours!

At all ages and stages, God's love will empower you to practice the tough as well as the tender love you need. Your human love will fall short many times, but His love never fails and is instantly available.

God is a Mediator. We have considered repeatedly the fact that disagreements in marriage and with children are inevitable. Power struggles that ensue are often destructive, and not every family can afford counseling or the services of a trained mediator.

Yet every family has instant access to the highest court in the universe. When you practice the presence of Christ, you will discover that He is there to mediate any disagreement and help you maintain harmony. Through giving the basic control over to God, you will avoid competing for authority. You can then develop the teamwork that creates a healthy family.

Positive Attitudes

"Whatever is true, whatever is honorable, whatever is right, whatever is pure, whatever is lovely, whatever is of good repute, if there is any excellence and if anything worthy of praise, let your mind dwell on these things" (Phil. 4:8, NASB). These words were written by the apostle Paul a long time ago.

Thousands of healthy families have discovered and practiced the truth of Paul's inspired words. They have listed an affirming, positive attitude as one of the top 10 values that have given them that health. Yet few indeed are those among us who can maintain such constructive thinking and attitudes on their own.

It is faith in God that will provide you with the power to stay positive even in the midst of the ever-recurring turbulence of family crises. Certainly the challenges of loss, grief, and disappointments are crises that will come to you. But God's Spirit will enable you to grow through these, not succumb to them.

When the apostle Paul struggled with his human weaknesses, he discovered this: "And He [Christ] said to me, 'My grace is sufficient for you, for My strength is made perfect in weakness.' Therefore most gladly I will rather boast in my infirmities, that the power of Christ may rest upon me" (2 Cor. 12:9, NKJV). In acknowledging our failures and weaknesses, we can find the true Source of real power in Jesus Christ. The highest level of joy and fulfillment both personally and in your marriage may be found through spiritual life and growth in God the Spirit.

How to Develop Spiritually

In the book *Marriage: First Things First,* you may have read about how to cultivate your Christian life. Let's review some of those principles.

Read God's Word

"Faith comes by hearing, and hearing by the word of God" (Rom. 10:17, NKJV). Many people find it laborious to study the Bible. If you are one of these, find a newer translation or paraphrase, such as *The Living Bible.* Once you read the Scriptures in today's English, you will find the Word indeed becomes the living Word.

Words are one of our best means of communicating with one another. It is no accident that God's Spirit inspired the writers of Scripture to call it the *Word.* It is God's clear teaching about all history and His presence and ultimate power throughout time. Certainly it is within that power to work redemption in each person and every family.

Talk with God

Prayer was once a ritual to me in which I implored God to hear me and obey my wishes or take my orders. In fact, I stumbled onto the awareness that I had developed the practice of begging God to do things He had already promised in His Word. One of the ritual prayers of a more formal church is this. Again and again the pastor speaks a request of God, and the congregation repeats, "Hear our prayer, O Lord!" Yet the Bible is filled with statements affirming that God hears our prayers and even knows our thoughts (Ps. 139:2). We need only to thank Him for being there for us.

I have learned (and must constantly refresh that knowledge) that prayer is a constant, inner conversation with God. As I drive to work, counsel with my patients, and struggle with the vicissitudes of life, I can talk aloud or silently with Him. Through this ongoing communication, I'm learning patience, transmitting His love, sharing His wisdom, and living joyfully. So can you!

Live with Nature

In today's busy metropolitan living we often lose sight of the greatest evidence of God's very existence. I've learned to watch the traffic very carefully as I drive. But that does not prevent my exhilaration as I see glimpses of the clearest blue sky emerging from the parting clouds. I watch for the flirting squirrels and hopping rabbits that live in my neighborhood. I even marvel at the sunlit gold of dandelion blossoms and the delicate majesty of purple wild violets along the sidewalks. Sometimes on my lunch break I walk to a tiny park and watch the birds that flock to a few crumbs I may drop. The first chapter of Romans makes it clear that God may be known through His creation. Explore it!

Know the Followers of Christ

It's true—there is a great deal of hypocrisy and many faults to be found among today's disciples of Jesus Christ. But there are so many who do exude His love and live out His compassion. When you know even a few of these people, you will know God a bit better.

Recently we celebrated the birth of our fourth grandson. As I helped with his care early in his life, I marveled all over again at the miracle of human life. His total helplessness and dependency reminded me of my own children, born long ago. But even more, he renewed my awareness of my complete dependency on my Heavenly Father for life now and for eternal life.

The mystical experience of life through birth is as old as mankind and as new as today. Certainly you may know God through the miracle of a child. I trust His divine gift will indeed become yours.

Postscript

As you can see, there are many areas of life you must evaluate to determine if you are ready for a child to enter your home. You may agree with me—if you were to wait for perfection in all of these, you might never have a child. In fact, the human race would have expired if everyone had insisted on the attainment of this lofty goal.

Forget perfection then! But do carefully look at yourselves as individuals and as a couple. Work out a plan to gain excellence in these areas:

1. Discipline your habits of eating, exercise, and rest in order to achieve the best possible physical health.
2. Learn to accept change, inconvenience, and even hardship in order to become a truly mature person.

3. Practice self-control and establish goals and long-range plans in order to enjoy economic security.
4. If you already have a child, prepare him or her as well as yourselves for a new baby.
5. Balance and modify your social activities in order to have time and energy to care for your new child.
6. Learn to think carefully, acquire accurate information, and make wise decisions.
7. Understand your emotions and express them with healthy control so you can teach your child to live with healthy emotions.
8. Perhaps you cannot have a child of your own. There are other avenues through which you can live out your parental yearnings.
9. Develop spiritual depth so you can find the wisdom and love that will empower your parenting.

May you know great joy in your role as parents!

Expectant Parents' Journal

Chapter 9

Getting in Touch

My *feelings* about the spiritual responsibility I will have toward my child are _____

_____

My *thoughts* about the spiritual responsibility I will have toward my child are _____

_____

Perception

List below 10 words that you could use to describe God's character.

_____	_____
_____	_____
_____	_____
_____	_____
_____	_____

Read 1 John 4:7-8 and 1 Cor. 13. Are the words and ideas used to describe God in these passages consistent with the 10 words you wrote above? How do these verses change your perception of God?

If you are listening, little one . . .

(Write a message to your unborn child.)

_____

_____

For Inspiration

But the fruit of the Spirit is love, joy, peace, patience, kindness, goodness, faithfulness, gentleness and self-control (Gal. 5:22-23).

Checkup!

Rate your faithfulness (good, fair, poor) in the following areas of spiritual maturity:

_____	Reading God's Word
_____	Talking with God
_____	Living with nature

_____ Fellowshipping with other fol-
lowers of Christ

List two things you will do this week to improve yourself in the above areas:

a.

b.

Accountability

List two or three Christian friends who you know will be interested in your spiritual growth. Thank God now for their influence and care in your life.

List two or three friends who you know need someone to be interested in their spiritual growth. Pray that you will be sensitive to God's leading for you in that friendship.

Goals

My desires for my child's spiritual growth as he or she matures are

a.

b.

c.

d.

Actions I can take that will enhance my child's opportunities to grow spiritually are

a.

b.

c.

d.

Notes